... Contents ...

KU-520-264

··· Easier Puzzles ···

Easier by the Dozen

Place the numbers from 1 through 12 as follows: The odd numbers go into the triangle. The even numbers go inside the circle. Any numbers that are divisible by three go into the square.

How will that look?

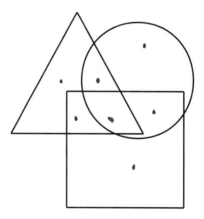

Hint on page 66.
Answer on page 91.

Waiting in Line

At the local sandwich shop, every customer who enters is given a number. During one particularly busy lunch hour, customers 17 through 31 were waiting to be called.

If you counted up all those waiting customers, how many would there be?

Hint on page 66.
Answer on page 91.

Who Is Faster?

Hector can run from the train station to his parents' house in eight minutes. His younger brother Darius can run the same distance eight times in one hour. (Not that he'd need to!) Who is faster?

Hint on page 66.
Answer on page 91.

4

Eggs-actly

If it takes three and a half minutes to boil an egg, how long does it take to boil four eggs? Be careful!

Hint on page 66.
Answer on page 91.

5

Double Trouble

It is possible to place the numbers 1 through 9 into the nine boxes below so that both of the multiplications in the sequence are correct. The numbers 3, 7, 8, and 9 have been placed for you. Can you figure out where the other five numbers go?

$$\boxed{}\boxed{8} \times \boxed{3} = \boxed{}\boxed{7}\boxed{} = \boxed{}\boxed{9} \times \boxed{}$$

Hint on page 67.
Answer on page 91.

6

Just Checking

Five kids sit down to play some games of checkers. If each of the five kids plays just one game with each of the others, what is the total number of games played?

Hint on page 67.
Answer on page 91.

7

Spreading the Word

Suppose you want to make copies of pages 12, 19, 30, 31, and 47 of a pocket dictionary. If it costs a dime to make one copy, how many dimes will you need?

Hint on page 67.
Answer on page 92.

Circular Reasoning

Only one of the four lines in the diagram shown here divides the circle into two equal parts. Can you find that line?

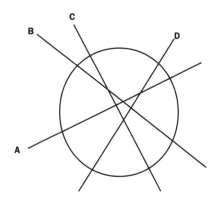

Hint on page 67.
Answer on page 92.

High-Speed Copying

If 4 copiers can process 400 sheets of paper in 4 hours, how long does it take 8 copiers to process 800 sheets?

Hint on page 68.
Answer on page 92.

If the Shoe Fits

A town has 20,000 people living in it. Five percent of them are one-legged, and half of the rest of them go barefoot. How many shoes are worn in the town?

Hint on page 68.
Answer on page 92.

An Odd Game of Bingo

Imagine playing a game of bingo using the card provided here, on which all the numbers are odd. The idea behind this particular game is that you must get a bingo—either across, up and down, or diagonally—that adds up to precisely 100. This can be done only one way. Do you see how?

23	11	25	15	41
1	37	31	5	17
9	21	FREE	27	47
43	35	33	29	7
19	45	3	39	13

Hint on page 68.
Answer on page 92.

12

One of a Kind

To write out the number FIFTEEN, you need seven letters. When you write out TEN, three letters are required. There is one and only one number for which the number of letters needed is the same as the number itself! Can you find that number?

Hint on page 68.
Answer on page 92.

13

The Long Road

If you perform all the operations that are indicated and end up with the number 97 in the circle, what number did you start with?

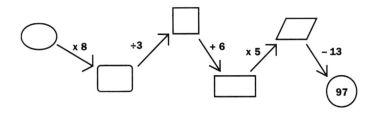

Hint on page 69.
Answer on page 93.

14

Store 24

Using the number 1 six times—and just three plus signs—can you form an expression that equals 24?

Hint on page 69.
Answer on page 93.

15

All in the Family

Each of the four Strickland brothers has a sister. Altogether, how many kids are in the family?

Hint on page 69.
Answer on page 93.

See You Later, Calculator

Which is bigger, 18 percent of 87 or 87 percent of 18? And don't multiply this out!

Hint on page 69.
Answer on page 93.

Strange but True

Melanie was given three positive numbers and told to add them up. Jessica was given the same three numbers and told to multiply them all together. Surprise, surprise: Melanie and Jessica got the same answer!

What numbers were they given?

Hint on page 69.
Answer on page 93.

We Can Work It Out

The dot-filled diagram is from an exercise bicycle at the health club. The numbers on the left stand for the degree of difficulty of the exercise. The higher the number, the greater the resistance offered by the bike, which increases the work-out. The columns represent time: Each column stands for 5, 10, or 15 seconds, depending on the total time chosen.

But we don't have to worry about all that, because our task is a mental challenge, not a physical one. How many dots are there in all?

One last piece of advice: Don't tackle the dots one by one; you'll just get dizzy. There's a better way!

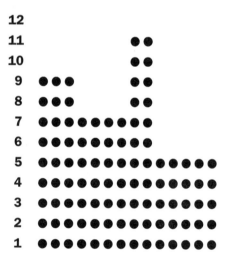

Hint on page 70.
Answer on page 93.

It's in the Bag

One bag contains three red marbles and two blue marbles. A second bag contains two red marbles and one blue marble. If you could pick only one marble, blindly, from one of the bags, what bag would you choose if you wanted to give yourself the best possible chance to pick a red marble?

Hint on page 70.
Answer on page 93.

He Was Framed!

Jennifer bought a picture frame for a 4" x 6" picture of her boyfriend. The outside of the frame measures 5" x 7". If the picture fits inside the opening perfectly, how wide is each border of the frame?

Hint on page 70.
Answer on page 94.

The Conversion Machine

If you give the conversion machine a number, it will put the number through three separate steps. First of all, the machine will divide the number by 5. Then it will multiply the new number by 9. Finally, the machine will subtract 32 from the result.

One of the following numbers remains the same after it has been put through all three stages of the conversion machine. Which one is it?

A)10   B)20   C)30   D)40

Hint on page 70.
Answer on page 94.

Say the Magic Words

Three favorite words of magicians are ABRACADABRA, PRESTO, and SHAZAM! If each letter is given a value from its position in the alphabet (A=1, B=2, and so on), and you add up the values for each word, which would have the highest value?

Hint on page 71.
Answer on page 94.

23

Incomplete Sentences

Place the appropriate sign (addition, subtraction, multiplication, or division) between the numbers 6, 3, and 2 to make the following number sentences true.

$$6 \quad 3 \quad 2 = 5$$

$$6 \quad 3 \quad 2 = 20$$

$$6 \quad 3 \quad 2 = 7$$

$$6 \quad 3 \quad 2 = 4$$

Hint on page 71.
Answer on page 95.

Switching Sides

Start with nine dots arranged in a square. The diagram here shows how to join some of the dots to form a figure with five sides. What is the greatest number of sides that a figure can have if formed in this way? the figure must be closed—no loose edges permitted.

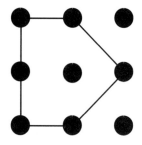

Hint on page 71.
Answer on page 95.

It All Adds Up

The sum of the digits of a certain three-digit number is 12. If the hundreds digit is three times the tens digit, and the tens digit is one-half the ones digit, what is the number?

Hint on page 71.
Answer on page 95.

Don't Sneeze, Please

If the doctor says to take an allergy pill every three hours, how much time will go by between the first pill and the fourth pill?

Hint on page 72.
Answer on page 95.

Forever Young

Heather was born in the winter of 1966. In April of 2006 she claimed to be only 39 years old. How can this be?

Hint on page 72.
Answer on page 95.

Agent 86

Fill in the missing squares in such a way that the rows, columns, and the two diagonals all add up to the same number.

32	19		8
10	25		
9			
35	16		11

Hint on page 72.
Answer on page 95.

Seeing Is Believing?

If you continued drawing the line that begins at the bottom left of the diagram, and kept going up, which line would you meet up with, A or B?

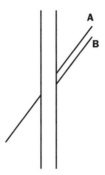

Hint on page 72.
Answer on page 96.

Five Easy Pieces

In the diagram, the big square is divided into four equal parts. Can you divide a square into five equal parts?

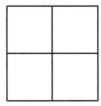

Hint on page 73.
Answer on page 96.

Follow the Directions

There are several different ways of placing the numbers 1 through 5 into the circles on the next page so that both directions—North/South and East/West—add up to the same number. But your question is a different one: Whatever way you happen to choose, the middle number will be the same; what is that number?

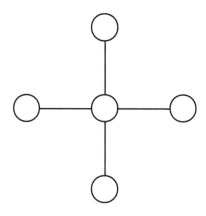

Hint on page 73.
Answer on page 96.

X Marks the Spot

Can you place five new Xs in the grid so that every row and column has an even number of Xs in it?

					X
	X	X			
	X				
	X				
X				X	
			X	X	

Hint on page 73.
Answer on page 96.

··· Medium Puzzles ···

33

The Price of Fun

A Frisbee® and a softball together cost $6.20. The Frisbee costs $1.20 more than the softball. How much does the Frisbee® cost?

Hint on page 73.
Answer on page 96.

34

Fare Wars

Suppose a taxicab in Megalopolis charges 75 cents for the first quarter-mile and 15 cents for each additional quarter-mile. In Cloud City, a taxi charges $1.00 for the first quarter-mile and 10 cents for each additional quarter-mile.

What distance would produce the same fare for the two taxicabs?

Hint on page 74.
Answer on page 96.

A Famous Triangle

The diagram shows the first six rows of a famous mathematical construction called Pascal's Triangle. The way the triangle works is that 1s are placed along the two outside edges, and each number within those edges is the sum of the two numbers above it. For example, the 6 in the middle of the fifth row is the sum of the two 3s from the fourth row.

Okay, now that you know what Pascal's Triangle is, what is the sum of all the elements of the unseen seventh row?

Note: You don't have to add up all the individual numbers in the seventh row in order to figure out their sum!

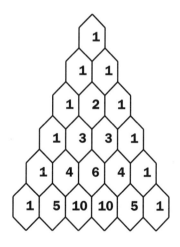

Hint on page 74.
Answer on page 97.

Magic Triangle

Here is an example of a "magic" triangle. What makes it magic is that the numbers on each of the three sides of the triangle add up to 12. Can you place the numbers from 1 through 6 in the blank triangle in such a way that each of the three sides of the new triangle adds up to 10?

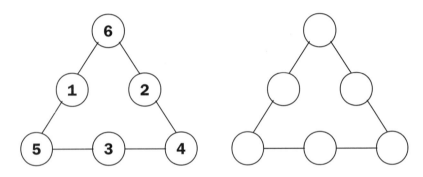

Hint on page 74.
Answer on page 97.

The French Connection

Jason and Sandy took five tests during their first year in French class. Jason's scores were 72, 85, 76, 81, and 91. Sandy's scores were 94, 79, 84, 75, and 88. How much higher was Sandy's average score than Jason's average score?

Hint on page 74.
Answer on page 98.

Numbers on the House

Suppose the town planning commission decides to buy brand-new house numbers for all of the residents of Sleepy Hollow Road. There are 50 houses on the road, numbered 1 through 50. How many of each number will they need?

Hint on page 75.
Answer on page 98.

Mirror Time

Below is the digital display of a clock reading four minutes after four. As you can see, the hour and minute figures are the same. It takes one hour and one minute before you see this pattern again—at 5:05.

What is the shortest possible time between two different readings of this same type?

4:04

Hint on page 75.
Answer on page 98.

Letter Perfect

Rearrange the letters in the phrase ELEVEN PLUS TWO to create a new phrase with the same meaning.

Hint on page 75.
Answer on page 98.

Prime Time

A number is called "prime" if its only factors are itself and 1. (Although 1 is not considered a prime number.) The first ten prime numbers are hidden in the square. Can you find them? We suggest taking a pencil and filling in every square that contains a prime number.

32	16	24	33	45	28	54
40	23	2	11	5	19	12
14	36	10	55	17	34	49
6	50	38	13	22	51	20
21	35	3	46	27	18	39
9	29	48	15	4	52	26
55	44	25	8	42	30	1

Hint on page 75.
Answer on page 98.

The Missing Six

Place the six numbers below into the empty circles so that both sentences are true. Use each number once and only once.

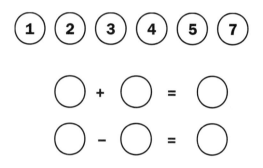

Hint on page 76.
Answer on page 99.

The One and Only

Believe it or not, there is only one number whose letters are in alphabetical order. Can you find it?

Hint on page 76.
Answer on page 99.

Comic Relief

While traveling in Russia, I bought six comic books for a total of 17 rubles. Some of the comics cost 1 ruble, others cost 2 rubles, while the most expensive ones sold for 10 rubles apiece.

How many of each type did I buy?

Hint on page 76.
Answer on page 99.

The Twelve Days of Christmas

The song "The Twelve Days of Christmas" includes some well-known presents:

A partridge in a pear tree
Two turtle doves
Three French hens
Four calling birds
Five golden rings
Six geese a-laying
Seven swans a-swimming
Eight maids a milking
Nine drummers drumming
Ten pipers piping
Eleven ladies dancing
Twelve lords a-leaping

Throughout the entire song, including all the twelve verses, which present shows up most often? (For example, "two turtle doves" counts as *two* presents every time that phrase is sung.)

Hint on page 76.
Answer on page 99.

Pickup Sticks

If you count out the matchsticks below, you'll see that the statement works out just fine. But can you rearrange the matchsticks so that the statement is still true and you don't need to do any counting?

$$| | | | | | | | | | | | | | | | | | | | | | | | | | | | | = 29$$

Hint on page 77.
Answer on page 99.

Starting to Waffle

A portable waffle machine makes 120 waffles per minute. A stationary waffle machine makes 3 waffles per second. How many portable machines would you need if you wanted to equal the output of four stationary machines?

Hint on page 77.
Answer on page 99.

And Then There Was One

Begin by crossing out the letter N. Now go around the circle, counter-clockwise, crossing out *every other* letter you pass. Once you have crossed out a letter, however, you do not count that letter as you go around the circle a second or third time. If you keep going in that fashion, what will be the last letter?

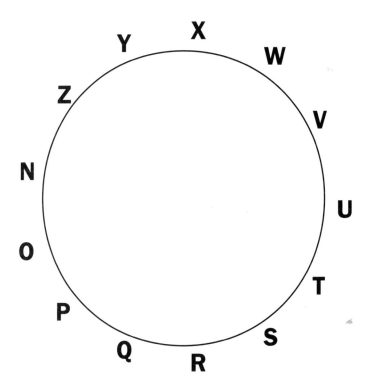

Hint on page 77.
Answer on page 99.

Class Dismissed

Suppose school starts promptly at 9:00 A.M. If each period lasts 40 minutes and there are 5 minutes between periods, when will the fourth period end?

Hint on page 77.
Answer on page 100.

The Easy Way Out

What is (138 x 109) + (164 x 138) + (138 x 227)? Can you answer without multiplying everything out?

Hint on page 78.
Answer on page 100.

An Updated Classic

Sixteen matchsticks have been arranged to form a backward "L." See if you can add eight matches to form a region separated into four identical smaller regions. It's a classic problem, but not everyone realizes that there are two completely different ways of solving it. Can you find one of those solutions?

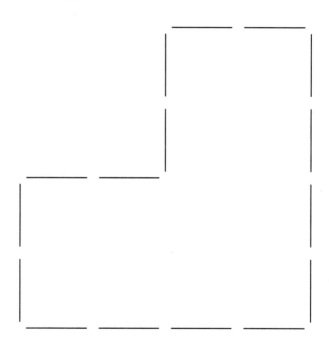

Hint on page 78.
Answer on page 100.

Generation Gap

Grandpa Jones has four grandchildren. Each grandchild is precisely one year older than the next oldest one. This year, Jones noticed that if you added the ages of his four grandchildren, you would get his own age. How old is Grandpa Jones now?

A) 76
B) 78
C) 80

Hint on page 78.
Answer on page 100.

A Game of Chicken

Chicken McNuggets come in packages of 6, 9, and 20. Suppose you wanted to purchase 99 McNuggets for you and your friends. Assuming you wanted to buy as few individual packages as possible, how many of each size would you order?

Hint on page 78.
Answer on page 100.

The Average Student

Melissa got a poor grade on her very first homework assignment at her new school—only one star out of a possible five stars! She was determined to do better. How many five-star ratings must she receive before she has an average rating of four stars?

Hint on page 79.
Answer on page 100.

Reel Life Story

A group of seven adults went to the movies. The total cost of the movie tickets was $30.00. This doesn't seem possible, does it? After all, 30 is not evenly divisible by 7. Ah, but there's a hitch. The reason that $30.00 was the total cost was that some members of the group were senior citizens, so they got to see the movie at half price.

How many of the group were senior citizens, and how much did the tickets cost?

Hint on page 79.
Answer on page 101.

Number Path

Place the numbers 1 through 20 into the grid so that they form a continuous chain. In other words, starting with 1, you must be able to get to 2 by going one space left, right, up, or down—although never diagonally—and so on, all the way to 20. Just make sure that the positions of 2, 7, 10, and 17 are just as you see them. There is only one solution. Can you find it?

	7	10		
	2		17	

Hint on page 79.
Answer on page 101.

Divide and Conquer

Fill in the boxes below to make the division problem work out.

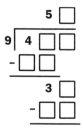

Hint on page 79.
Answer on page 101.

Apple Picking

Seventh Heaven Orchards decides to hold a special sale at the end of the season, hoping that people will come and buy the apples that have already fallen from the trees. They decide on an unusual system for pricing the apples. The bags they give out hold just seven apples each. The orchard then charges its customers 5 cents for every full bag of apples— and 15 cents for every apple left over! According to the system, which costs the most: 10 apples, 30 apples, or 50 apples?

Hint on page 80.
Answer on page 101.

Squaring the Circle

In the diagram, a circle is nested inside a large square and then a smaller square is tilted and nested inside the circle. How big is the tilted square in relation to the larger one?

Hint on page 80.
Answer on page 101.

Where's Waldo?

Waldo is in the fourth grade. In Waldo's class, everyone sits in the same chair every day, and there are the same number of kids in every row. One day, a substitute teacher came in and asked Waldo where he sat. He was too shy to answer, so several of his classmates answered for him:

Maria said, "Waldo sits in the third row."
Jerry said, "Waldo sits in the fourth row from the back."
Alice said, "Waldo sits in the second seat from the right."
Oliver said, "Waldo sits in the fourth seat from the left."

How many students are in the class?

Hint on page 80.
Answer on page 101.

Hundred's Place

Suppose the skyscraper pattern you see here kept going and going. Would the number 100 belong in a short column, a medium column, or a tall column? Can you figure this out without writing out all the numbers in between?

	6			12	
3	5		9	11	
1	2	4	7	8	10

Hint on page 80.
Answer on page 102.

The Powers of Four

Bert and Ernie take turns multiplying numbers. First Bert chooses the number 4. Ernie multiplies it by 4 to get 16. Bert multiplies that by 4 to get 64. Ernie multiplies that by 4 to get 256.

After going back and forth several times, one of them comes up with the number 1,048,576. Who came up with that number, Bert or Ernie?

Don't worry—the problem is easier than it looks at first glance. You don't have to multiply out the whole thing to figure out the correct answer!

Hint on page 81.
Answer on page 102.

Kangaroo Numbers

A kangaroo number is a number of two digits or more that shows one of its factors. The digits of the factor have to appear in order within the number. Easy kangaroos to spot are any numbers with a zero at the end—for example, 560, which has its factor of 56 appearing inside. (Of course, 5 also divides evenly into 560, but it is only one digit long; 65 is another factor, but the digits appear in reversed order.)

Now that you know how they work, which of the following numbers are kangaroo numbers?

A) 125   B) 664   C) 729   D) 912

Hint on page 81.
Answer on page 102.

Hex-a-Gone

Drawing just three lines, can you transform the hexagon into a cube?

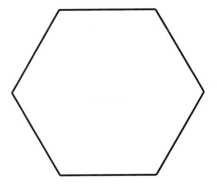

Hint on page 81.
Answer on page 102.

Staying in Shape

The figure below shows one way to join four squares at the edges to make a solid shape. How many different shapes can be created out of four squares? (Two shapes are not considered different if one can simply be rotated to produce the other.)

Hint on page 81.
Answer on page 102

Oh, Brother!

Jeff was watching his older brother Matt do his math homework. Matt said that the assignment was about factorials, a subject much too complex for Jeff to understand.

"What's the exclamation point?" Jeff asked, looking at the strange expression 8! In the middle of his brother's notes.

"It's a factorial symbol," Matt said.

"Well, what's a factorial?" Jeff asked.

Matt said, "A factorial is when you take all the whole numbers less than or equal to a particular number and multiply them all together. So 10! = 10 x 9 x 8 x 7 x 6 x 5 x 4 x 3 x 2 x 1. Now do you believe me when I say these things are hard?"

"I guess so," Jeff said. "But what's the problem you're working on?"

"I have to figure out what 8! divided by 6! is," Matt said.

Two seconds later, Jeff said, "I see the answer."

How did Jeff figure out what 8!/6! was without multiplying the whole thing out before dividing it?

Hint on page 81.
Answer on page 102.

Crossing the Bridge

In the game of bridge, a standard deck of 52 playing cards is dealt evenly among four people. The cards held by a particular player are called that player's "hand." Players assign a value to their hands by counting 4 points for an ace, 3 points for a king, 2 points for a queen, and 1 point for a jack. Sorry, but you don't get points for any other card.

Suppose that you are dealt a hand with one ace, three 7s, two 5s, and two 4s. Even without looking at your other cards, what is the greatest number of points you could possibly have in your hand?

Hint on page 82.
Answer on page 103

.

Last Train to Clarksville

Brian, Amy, and Stephanie are waiting at the train station. Each of the three is waiting for a different train. When they check the station clock, they realize that Amy is going to have to wait twice as long for her train as Brian will for his, while Stephanie will have to wait twice as long as Amy!

What time is it?

DESTINATION	TRACK	DEPARTURE
NEWBURGH	3	4:48
SPRINGFIELD	7	4:57
CLARKSVILLE	4	5:15

Hint on page 82.
Answer on page 103.

··· Harder Puzzles ···

How Big?

In the figure below, we have drawn lines from each corner of a square to the midpoint of one of the opposite sides. How big is the smaller square in the middle—relative to the original square?

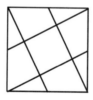

Hint on page 82.
Answer on page 103.

Putting Your Two Cents In

Many years ago, when things cost a whole lot less than they do today, two brothers—Aaron and Bobby—went to the corner drugstore to purchase a pad of paper. Unfortunately, although both brothers had money, neither brother had much. Aaron realized that he was 2 cents short of the price of the pad, while Bobby was 24 cents short. When they put their money together, they found that they still didn't have enough to purchase the pad!

How much does the pad cost?

Hint on page 83.
Answer on page 103.

Connect the Dots

Can you place just ten dots on a page using five lines of four dots apiece?

Hint on page 83.
Answer on page 103.

Surf's Up

At a surf shop in Malibu, California, a used blue surfboard is
on sale for $100.00. According to the salesperson, the new
price represents a 20% discount from the original price. What
did it sell for originally?

Hint on page 83.
Answer on page 104.

Square Dance

First count up the number of squares in the figure. Can you
remove just four line segments to cut the total number of
squares in half?

Don't leave any segments "hanging." Every segment must
be part of at least one square.

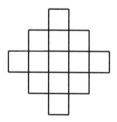

Hint on page 83.
Answer on page 104.

On All Fours

Using just basic addition, subtraction, multiplication, and division, can you produce sums equal to each of the numbers from 1 through 10 using precisely four 4s?

To give you an idea of how this works, we'll start you off:

$$1 = (4 + 4)/(4 + 4)$$
$$2 = (4 \times 4)/(4 + 4)$$

The rest is up to you!

Hint on page 83.
Answer on page 104.

The Right Stuff

Ninety people applied for a job as a salesperson for a book publishing company. Ten of the applicants had never worked in sales or in the publishing business. Sixty-five had worked in sales at some point, and fifty-eight had some background in publishing.

How many of the applicants had experience in *both* sales and publishing?

Hint on page 83.
Answer on page 104.

Square Feet

A group of fewer than 100 soldiers was marching in a square formation when 32 of them were called off for a training mission. The remaining soldiers regrouped and continued their marching, this time forming a smaller square. They continued to march until eight of them had to leave to run an obstacle course.

How many soldiers were there originally?

Hint on page 84.
Answer on page 104.

Win One for the Dipper

Can you draw three straight lines in the diagram below so that each star of the Big Dipper lies in its own separate region within the rectangle?

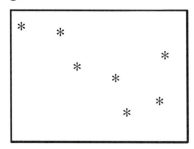

Hint on page 84.
Answer on page 104.

Trick or Treat

Halloween night was almost over, and fewer than 20 candies remained at the Greensleeve household. When the doorbell rang, Mr. Greensleeve figured it was the final group of trick-or-treaters for the night, so he decided to give away the rest of his candy.

At the door were two kids, one dressed as a ghost and the other as a lion. Mr. Greensleeve wanted to give them both the same number of candies, but he noticed that when he split the candies up, there was one left over.

At that point he noticed that a witch was hiding behind the lion. Now there were three trick-or-treaters. He tried dividing the candies equally among the three, but, again, one candy was left over.

Finally, Dracula jumped out from behind the ghost. Mr. Greensleeve tried dividing the candies among the *four* trick-or-treaters, but again there was one left over.

How many candies did Mr. Greensleeve have when the doorbell rang?

Hint on page 84.
Answer on page 105.

Magic Circle

The numbers 1 through 9 are arranged in a circle. Can you divide the numbers into three groups—not changing the order—so that the sum of the numbers in each group is the same?

Hint on page 84.
Answer on page 105.

Jack in the Box

Of six cards from a full deck of playing cards, two are jacks. Suppose you placed all six cards in a box and selected two at random. Which is more likely—that you will select at least one jack or that you will select no jacks at all?

Hint on page 85.
Answer on page 105.

81

Three's a Charm

There is an inexpensive item that can be purchased for less than one U.S. dollar. You could buy it with four standard U.S. coins and get no change. If you wanted to buy two of these items with exact change, you'd need at least six coins. However, if you bought three, you'd only need two coins. How much does the item cost?

Recall that you have only five U.S. coins to work with that are less than one dollar: A penny (1 cent), a nickel (5 cents), a dime (10 cents), a quarter (25 cents), and a half-dollar (50 cents).

Hint on page 85.
Answer on page 105.

82

Miles to Go

The "odometer" of a car tells you how far it has traveled in its lifetime. The "trip odometer" can be reset at any time to tell you the length of a particular trip. Suppose the main odometer of a new car is at 467 and the trip odometer is at 22. How many more miles do you have to travel before the main odometer is precisely two times the trip odometer?

Hint on page 85.
Answer on page 106.

Stay Out of My Path!

The idea of this puzzle is to connect the four pairs of similar squares: the gray with the gray, the X mark with the X mark, and so on. But can you connect the four pairs so that none of the four pathways crosses any of the others?

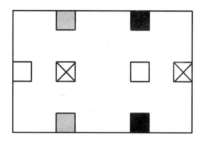

Hint on page 85.
Answer on page 106.

The Run-Off

In a 10-kilometer race, Alex beat Burt by 20 meters and Carl by 40 meters. If Burt and Carl were to run a 10-K race, and Burt were to give Carl a 20-meter head start, who would probably win?

Hint on page 86.
Answer on page 106.

The Missing Shekel

The farmer in ancient Transylvania took his rutabagas to market each week. His standard price was three rutabagas for a shekel. On an average week, he sold 30 rutabagas and came home with 10 shekels.

One week, he agreed to sell the rutabagas grown by his neighbor, who wasn't feeling well enough to make the trip into town. The only surprise was that the neighbor's preferred price was two rutabagas for a shekel. When the neighbor sold 30 rutabagas, he came home with 15 shekels.

The farmer decided the only fair thing to do was to sell the combined crop at the rate of five rutabagas for two shekels. But when he added up his money after selling both his crop and his neighbor's crop, he had only 24 shekels, not the 25 he was expecting.

What happened to the missing shekel?

Hint on page 86.
Answer on page 106.

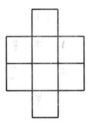

Too Close for Comfort

See if you can place the numbers 1 through 8 in the boxes below so that no two consecutive numbers are touching—either horizontally, vertically, or diagonally!

Hint on page 86.
Answer on page 107.

Donut Try This at Home

Suppose a low-calorie donut has 95 percent fewer calories than a regular donut. How many low-calorie donuts would you need to eat to take in as many calories as you'd get from a regular donut?

Hint on page 86.
Answer on page 107.

Diamond in the Rough

Of the four suits that make up a deck of cards, only the diamonds are symmetrical, in that a diamond—unlike a club, a
heart, or a spade—looks the same whether it is rightside-up
or upside-down.

However, one of the 13 diamond cards is different when
you turn it upside-down. Without checking any decks of cards
you may have lying around, can you name that one non-sym-
metrical diamond?

Hint on page 86.
Answer on page 107.

Please Fence Me In

Suppose you had a long stretch of fencing with which to make
a nice big playpen for your new puppy, Sam. If you wanted to
give Sam the biggest possible area to roam around in, what
shape should the fence be?

Hint on page 87.
Answer on page 107.

Misery Loves Company

Two investors—we'll call them Smith and Jones—made some unfortunate decisions in the stock market: Smith lost 60% of his money and Jones lost 85%. Jones was so discouraged he took his money out and put it into a savings bank. Smith, on the other hand, made some additional investments in an effort to get his money back. But he wasn't any luckier the second time around—he lost another 60%!

Well, neither of them made a very strong showing, that much is certain. But who did worse, Smith or Jones?

Hint on page 87.
Answer on page 107.

Square Route

Four dots are arranged in a square. Starting at the upper left dot, draw three straight lines, each line going through one or more dots, so that you end up where you started. Every dot should have a line going through it.

•   •

•   •

Hint on page 87.
Answer on page 107.

Cookie Monster

A bag contains three cookies and each of them is different: one chocolate chip, one oatmeal raisin, and one sugar cookie. Elmo reaches in and picks one cookie, then Peter does the same. Who has the better chance of ending up with the sugar cookie—Elmo, who went first, or Peter, who went second?

Hint on page 87.
Answer on page 108.

Two Workers Are Better Than One

If one worker can complete a job in 6 days and a second worker takes 12 days to complete the same job, how long will it take them working together?

Hint on page 88.
Answer on page 108.

Four of a Kind

Divide the figure below into four identical pieces.

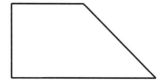

Hint on page 88.
Answer on page 109.

No Foolin'

In the year 2000, April 1 (called April Fool's Day in many parts of the world) took place on a Saturday. On what day was April 1, 1999? What about April 1, 2001?

Hint on page 88.
Answer on page 109.

A Very Good Year

The year 1978 has an unusual property. When you add the 19 to the 78, you get 97—the middle two digits of the year! What will be the next year to have this same property?

Hint on page 89.
Answer on page 109.

Pieces of Eight

An octagon is an eight-sided figure. A stop sign is perhaps the most familiar example of a "regular" octagon, in which all eight sides have the same length. Inside the regular octagon on the next page, we have drawn three diagonals—lines connecting two of the extreme points. How many diagonals are there in all?

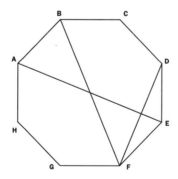

Hint on page 89.
Answer on page 109.

Who Is the Liar?

Four friends—Andrew, Barbara, Cindy, and Daniel—were shown a number. Here's what they had to say about that number:

> Andrew: "It has two digits."
> Barbara: "It goes evenly into 150."
> Cindy: "It is not 150."
> Daniel: "It is divisible by 25."

It turns out that one (and only one) of the four friends is lying. Which one is it?

Hint on page 89.
Answer on page 109.

Playing the Triangle

The triangle in the diagram has the lengths of two sides labeled. The reason the third side isn't labeled is that the labeler couldn't remember whether it was 5 units long, 11 units long, or 21 units long. Can you figure out which it is? (Sorry, but the diagram is *not* drawn to scale!)

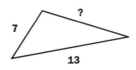

Hint on page 89.
Answer on page 110.

House of Cards

In the diagram shown, nine playing cards are set up to form a rectangle. Assuming that the area of the rectangle is 180 square inches, what is its perimeter? (The perimeter is the distance around the entire rectangle.)

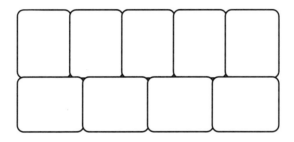

Hint on page 90.
Answer on page 110.

··· Hints ···

1

Easier by the Dozen

The puzzle would not be possible if the triangle, circle, and square didn't overlap. Pay careful attention to the placement of numbers that are multiples of 3—namely, 3, 6, 9, and 12.

2

Waiting in Line

Careful, the answer is not 14.

3

Who Is Faster?

First figure how long it takes Hector to run the distance eight times.

4

Eggs-actly

When the problem asked you to be careful, that was a warning to watch out for a trick!

5
Double Trouble

You can figure out the ones digit of the three-digit number from the information you have already. (That's the sixth box from the left.) Then try and figure out the missing number on the far left.

6
Just Checking

Remember, if Ted plays against Jennifer, Jennifer is also playing against Ted! If you like, you can use A, B, C, D, and E for the kids, and then list all the one-on-one match-ups.

7
Spreading the Word

Another trick question—will they never stop?! Just make sure to take a close look at the page numbers of the pocket dictionary.

8
Circular Reasoning

In order for a line to divide the circle into two equal parts, that line must go through the center of the circle.

9

High-Speed Copying

Questions with this same pattern have been around for a lot longer than copiers! The best approach is to look at the number of copies an individual machine can make, and go on from there.

10

If the Shoe Fits

Read the puzzle carefully. It might interest you to know that the number five—as in 5%—doesn't really have much to do with the solution.

11

An Odd Game of Bingo

Some of the rows contain numbers too big to add up to just 100. But there's another clue: Is 100 odd or even? Is the sum of four odd numbers odd or even? What about five odd numbers? You don't have to do much actual addition to solve this problem, because answering those questions can rule out many of the answers before you even begin!

12

One of a Kind

Fortunately, the number you're looking for isn't all that big. But you suspected that, right?

13
The Long Road

This problem has to be done backward. Work from right to left, and do the opposite of what you're told to do!

14
Store 24

All you have to do is look at the groups of 1s another way.

15
All in the Family

The puzzle states that each of the brothers has a sister. It doesn't say that each of the brothers has a *different* sister.

16
See You Later, Calculator!

Remember, you don't need to make any calculations to solve this one—or have you forgotten the title already? Common sense is the winner here.

17
Strange but True

As a general rule, the bigger the numbers you choose, the greater the difference will be between their sum and their product.

18

We Can Work It Out

The problem is best tackled by separating the dots into rectangles. Just figure out the number of dots in each rectangle, then add them up.

19

It's in the Bag

The idea is to calculate the two probabilities as fractions, then to compare those fractions.

20

He Was Framed!

This is a trick question. The answer is not 1 inch.

21

The Conversion Machine

This one is pretty simple. Just follow the same rules as the machine, and you'll find the magic number.

22

Say the Magic Words

Just because a word is long that doesn't mean its "value" is high. Check out all the A's in ABRACADABRA!

23

Incomplete Sentences

Remember that you perform the various operations (addition, subtraction, multiplication, division) from left to right.

24

Switching Sides

Trial and error is the best approach. Remember that you don't have to use each and every dot.

25

It All Adds Up

You know that the tens digit is divisible by 3 but is no higher than 9 (since the most *any* single digit can be is 9). So you don't have that many choices.

26

Don't Sneeze, Please

Another trick question. Read it carefully, and put yourself in the position of the person who is taking the pills—even if you don't have allergies!

27

Forever Young

Another trick question. We never said where Heather lives.

28

Agent 86

If you add up the numbers in the first column, you will find out the sum for every row, column, or diagonal. Then go on to those rows or columns containing three out of the four possible numbers, and you'll be able to figure out the missing number. Pretty soon you'll be all done!

29

Seeing Is Believing?

Try looking at the diagram at an angle.

30

Five Easy Pieces

Don't forget the title. Whatever you do, you don't want to make this one harder than it really is.

31

Follow the Directions

You can solve the puzzle by trial and error, and the middle number of any solution is the middle number of *every* solution! But there's also a common sense approach that might give you the answer without placing numbers in all five positions.

32

X Marks the Spot

By definition, each row and column must have either two or four Xs in it. Remember, it's *even* not *equal*!

33

The Price of Fun

You don't need algebra to solve this puzzle, though it would help. A little trial and error should see you through, but you'd better make sure that the difference between the cost of the two items is $1.20.

Fare Wars

What is the initial cost difference between the two cabs? How does that difference then change every quarter-mile?

A Famous Triangle

See if you can find a pattern in the sums of the first six rows.

Magic Triangle

The key to the puzzle is figuring out the corner numbers. In the example given, the three biggest numbers are placed in the corners, where they count twice. So the sum of each leg is as big as possible (12), given the set of numbers being used. To get 10 or a smaller number, start by making a change to those corners.

The French Connection

You can figure out the average grade for each student by adding up the individual test scores and dividing by five. But if you look closely at the test scores, you may find a shortcut.

38
Numbers on the House

Count them up by considering the tens place and the ones place individually. Then put the totals together.

39
Mirror Time

There are twelve such times during each twelve-hour span. Going from 1:01 to 2:02 takes one hour and one minute; same for going from 2:02 to 3:03. But there is one occasion when the time gets shorter.

40
Letter Perfect

The new phrase also consists of three words, and one of them is left unchanged!

41
Prime Time

At first glance, there are only nine prime numbers in the diagram. But if you follow the directions carefully, you might find the tenth one.

The Missing Six

More trial and error. If the 7 in the puzzle was replaced by a 6, no answer would be possible. Since 7 is the highest number, it's most likely a sum or the number being subtracted from in one equation.

The One and Only

Trial and error will get you there! The answer has more than one digit, which is a clue. And you should be able to rule out two-digit numbers in bunches.

Comic Relief

First ask yourself, how many 10-ruble comic books can there be?

The Twelve Days of Christmas

Forget about the partridge. He appears the most often, but only comes one at a time!

46
Pickup Sticks

Twenty-nine is an unusual number. No other number would work in its place in this problem. Note, for example, that it doesn't have an "o" in it!

47
Starting to Waffle

Translate the rate of the portable machine into waffles per second. That way you can compare the two rates directly.

48
And Then There Was One

Just keep going, and don't forget that once a letter has been crossed out, it has disappeared for the purposes of this puzzle. And use a pencil!

49
Class Dismissed

Don't forget that the number of periods and the number of breaks between periods are not the same!

50
The Easy Way Out

Don't perform the indicated multiplication. Note that 138 is repeated in all three expressions. Even better, the other numbers add up to a nice round number.

51
An Updated Classic

One of the solutions occurs within the "L" shape, while the other ventures outside.

52
Generation Gap

Trial and error may work out here. You also might save some time if you notice that one of the three ages has a property that the other two do not have.

53
A Game of Chicken

Try subtracting 6s and 9s from 99 until you get a multiple of 20.

54

The Average Student

Knowing that the average of the ratings must be four, you start out with a three-point difference between the one-star rating (given to Melissa on her first assignment) and the desired four-star average. Well, how many stars can you make up at a time?

55

Reel Life Story

Trial and error will win the day. Note that the price of a senior ticket must divide evenly into 30.

56

Number Path

You won't have much trouble figuring out where 8 and 9 go. From there it's on to 6, 5, and so on. Be careful not to back yourself into a corner.

57

Divide and Conquer

Start by multiplying the 5 and the 9 to get the second row of the division. That should get you rolling.

58

Apple Picking

There is nothing tricky about the calculations here, but the answer may be a surprise.

59

Squaring the Circle

Often, you can see answers to puzzles like this one by drawing extra lines. Try drawing two diagonals in the tilted square and see if that helps!

60

Where's Waldo?

Drawing a diagram is one way to get the solution. Don't forget that there is an equal number of students in each row—without that information, you couldn't figure out the total number of students.

61

Hundred's Place

Note that the top number in each of the tall columns is a multiple of 6. If you use this pattern, you can predict what happens around the number 100 without writing out all the numbers.

62
The Powers of Four

If you kept multiplying by 4, that would lead you to the right answer, but an easier approach is to look for patterns.

63
Kangaroo Numbers

Remember that an even number cannot possibly divide evenly into an odd number. This will help you reduce the number of possibilities.

64
Hex-a-Gone

Try separating the hexagon into three diamond-shaped pieces and see what happens.

65
Staying in Shape

Pencil and paper are really required for this one.

66
Oh, Brother!

Don't worry about the exclamation point. You don't have to multiply out either 8! or 6!, but you do need to see that "cancellation" makes the problem easier.

67

Crossing the Bridge

Remember, a deck of cards consists of four suits of 13 cards apiece. There are only four aces, and the same holds true for kings, queens, and jacks.

68

Last Train to Clarksville

The first step is to figure out how much time goes by between the departures of the various trains. There is only one possibility for the current time.

69

How Big?

Try putting together the shapes that surround the central square.

70

Putting Your Two Cents In

The fact that the pad doesn't cost much is important to the solution, because many people tend to overlook the actual solution.

71
Connect the Dots

The answer is actually a very familiar shape.

72
Surf's Up

A common guess is $120.00, but that's not right.

73
Square Dance

Remember when you're counting up all the squares, you need to include squares of different sizes.

74
On All Fours

It might help to know that you can create 0 by using the number four twice (4 – 4) and create the number 1 a similar way (4/4). These are useful building blocks in making the numbers 1 through 10.

75
The Right Stuff

If you add up all the numbers, you'll get something way too big. But you're on the right track as long as you *subtract* the right number from your total.

76

Square Feet

The question is, what number is a perfect square and stays a perfect square when you subtract 32 from it? Don't worry, since the number of soldiers is less than 100, the number of soldiers on either side of the square is a single-digit number. But remember that the second square must have more than eight men in it.

77

Win One for the Dipper

Use a ruler and use pencil! Also, you might want to look at the page from an angle, just to make sure that you can draw a line through certain spaces.

78

Trick or Treat

Remember, Mr. Greensleeve has fewer than 20 candies remaining, and many possibilities can be ruled out immediately. Try listing the numbers from 1 to 20 and crossing them out as you go along.

79

Magic Circle

First figure out the sum of all nine numbers. Divide that sum by 3, and you have the sum of each of the three smaller groups.

Jack in the Box

Count out all the possibilities and see how many involve no jacks.

Three's a Charm

It's probably easiest to look at the combinations of two coins. What combinations of two coins produce a number that is divisible by 3? For example, a quarter plus a penny equals 26 cents, which is not divisible by 3, so this combination can be ruled out. On the other hand, a nickel plus a penny equals 6 cents, which is divisible by 3 but isn't nearly big enough to satisfy the problem! Once you get the right combination of two coins, you can work backward to get the rest of the answer.

Miles to Go

What is the gap between the two odometers?

Stay Out of My Path!

Two of the routes are fairly direct, but the other two are long and windy. Try to use space wisely. Don't crowd yourself out. It's okay for two paths to run alongside each other for a stretch, but they must not cross.

The Run-Off

It's a trick question. The trick is to see that the race between Burt and Carl will not be a tie.

The Missing Shekel

Is the price of five rutabagas for two shekels as fair as it looks?

Too Close for Comfort

The two boxes in the middle hold the key to the solution. Since the idea of the puzzle is to keep close numbers far apart, you might want to start by making sure that the numbers in the two middle boxes are far apart!

Donut Try This at Home

If a regular donut has, say, 100 calories, how many does a low-calorie donut have?

Diamond in the Rough

The idea is to visualize how the diamonds are put on the cards. The only hint you'll need is that there are never three diamonds in a row across the card, although for the higher numbers there are certainly three or more diamonds in a row going down the card.

89
Please Fence Me In

All that you need for this one is common sense. You're not being asked to come up with proof that one shape is best. Now that would be tougher!

90
Misery Loves Company

Suppose they each started out with one thousand dollars. After the first losses, Smith had $400.00 and Jones had $150.00. Now you have to work out how much Smith had left after his second 60% loss. (We are not including any interest that Jones might have earned from his savings account.)

91
Square Route

All three lines go beyond the boundary of the square.

92
Cookie Monster

As with many puzzles, you can solve this one by using numbers or common sense or both. What if there was a third person? What would that third person's chances be of ending up with the sugar cookie?

93

Two Workers Are Better Than One

One way to figure out the problem is to find out what portion of the job each worker accomplishes in one day. But if you don't want to work with fractions, just ask what the two workers would accomplish in 12 days—working together, of course.

94

Four of a Kind

If you divide the figure in the following way, you can see that the total area equals six small squares (five are intact, and the other two pieces combine to make the sixth one). So if you want to divide this figure into four equal pieces, the size of each piece must be 61/44 = 111/42 small squares. Go from there!

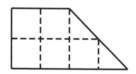

95

No Foolin'

There are 365 days in most years, almost precisely 52 weeks. Almost. The fact that 365 is not evenly divisible by 7 is at the heart of the problem.

96

A Very Good Year

The year could not be in the 2000s or the 2100s, because then the two-digit *middle* number never could be higher than the *first* two digits. So start with the year 2200 and work from there. You need to do a little trial and error—but not too much!

97

Pieces of Eight

Be sure not to "double-count" the diagonals. The diagonal joining A to E is the same as the diagonal joining E to A.

98

Who Is the Liar?

First assume that Andrew is lying, and see if it is possible for Barbara, Cindy, and Daniel to all be telling the truth. Then do the same for the other three. In only one case will there be only one liar.

99

Playing the Triangle

It is not possible to take just any three numbers and form a triangle with those numbers as the lengths of the sides. Remember, the shortest path between two points is a straight line.

House of Cards

Figure out the dimensions of each card first.

··· Solutions ···

1 Easier by the Dozen

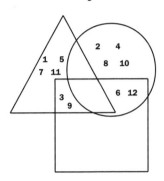

2 Waiting in Line

It's easy to guess 14, from 31 − 17, but the actual answer is 15 customers. To see why, suppose that only people with the numbers 17, 18, and 19 were waiting. You know that 19 − 17 = 2, but you also know that there are three customers, not two. The general rule is that you must subtract the two numbers and then add one.

3 Who Is Faster?

Hector can run a mile in eight minutes, so it takes him 64 minutes to run eight miles. But Darius can run eight miles in just 60 minutes, so Darius is faster. There might be another question here. Could Hector keep up his eight-minute pace for an entire hour? Maybe, maybe not. However, if he can't keep up that pace, it just proves that Darius is faster!

4 Eggs-actly

Did you check the hint to see that it was a trick question? If the pot of water is big enough, four eggs can all be boiled at the same time, so it takes three and a half minutes to boil four eggs—same as with just one!

5 Double Trouble

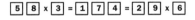

6 Just Checking

Each of the five kids plays four games, so it looks as though there must have been 5 x 4 = 20 games played in all. But wait! The game that Simon played against Theodore (for example) is the same game that Theodore played against Simon. You can't count a game twice. The actual number of games played equals 20/2 = 10 games.

Looking at it another way, suppose the first player plays each of the others, for a total of 4 games. Then the second player plays the 3 remaining players (other than player #1), and so on. You get a total of 4 + 3 + 2 + 1 = 10 games.

7 Spreading the Word

Four dimes are enough. In traditional page numbering, pages 30 and 31 always are on the same spread, which means they face each other. In the problem, it is a pocket dictionary and therefore small in size, so two facing pages could easily be copied on the same sheet.

8 Circular Reasoning

Line C divides the circle into two equal pieces. It is the only line that goes through the center of the circle.

9 High-Speed Copying

Eight copiers can process 800 sheets in 4 hours. Doubling the number of copiers will double the output without changing the amount of time required.

10 If the Shoe Fits

The total number of shoes is 20,000, the same as the total population of the town. That's because the one-legged people wear one shoe, while half of the remaining people wear two shoes and half wear no shoes at all. That's an average of one shoe per person.

11 An Odd Game of Bingo

23	11	25	15	41
1	37	31	5	17
9	21	FREE	27	47
43	35	33	29	7
19	45	3	39	13

12 One of a Kind

The number is FOUR.

13 The Long Road

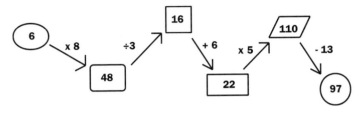

14 Store 24

$11 + 11 + 1 + 1 = 24$

15 All in the Family

There are five kids in the family: four boys and one girl. Each of the brothers has a sister, all right—but they share the same one!

16 See You Later, Calculator!

The solution is that 18 percent of 87 equals 87 percent of 18. Written as equations, 18 percent of 87 is $(18/100) \times 87$ and 87 percent of 18 is $(87/100) \times 18$. You don't have to do any multiplication or division to see that these two expressions are equal, simply because the same numbers—87 and 18—are used in the same actions in both.

17 Strange but True

The numbers are 1, 2, and 3. It's easy to check: $1 + 2 + 3 = 1 \times 2 \times 3 = 6$.

18 We Can Work It Out

The total number of dots equals 102. The easiest way is to separate the dots into four rectangles. Group the first three columns into one rectangle that's 3 dots wide by 9 dots tall, then continue: 4 x 7, 2 x 11, and 5 x 5. That produces $27 + 28 + 22 + 25 = 102$ dots.

19 It's in the Bag

Pick the second bag. The second bag gives you a 2/3 chance of picking a red marble, while the chance of a red marble from the first bag is only 3/5. (To see that 2/3 is greater than 3/5, find the common denominator of 15: $2/3 = 10/15$ and $3/5 = 9/15$.)

20 He Was Framed!

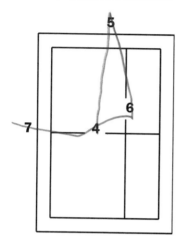

As long as you didn't answer too fast, this one wasn't all that tough. The trick is not to answer one inch. The width of the picture frame was ½ of an inch—remember, the frame goes around all four sides of the picture!

21 The Conversion Machine

The only number to stay the same after being put through the conversion machine is the number 40. You can see that 40/5 = 8, 8 x 9 = 72, and 72 – 32 = 40.

In real life, the conversion machine is similar to the transfor-

mation between two different temperature scales—the Fahrenheit scale and the Celsius (Centigrade) scale. The difference is that the only temperature to be the same in the Fahrenheit and Celsius scales is 40 degrees *below* zero—when we're too cold to care!

22 Say the Magic Words

The values of the magic words are as follows:

ABRACADABRA = 1 + 2 + 18 + 1 + 3 + 1 + 4 + 1 + 2 + 18 + 1 = 52
PRESTO = 16 + 18 + 5 + 19 + 20 + 15 = 93
SHAZAM = 19 + 8 + 1 + 26 + 1 + 13 = 68

As you can see, PRESTO has the highest value. Even though ABRACADABRA is the longest word by far, it has the lowest value.

23 Incomplete Sentences

$$\boxed{6} - \boxed{3} + \boxed{2} = 5$$

$$\boxed{6} \times \boxed{3} + \boxed{2} = 20$$

$$\boxed{6} + \boxed{3} - \boxed{2} = 7$$

$$\boxed{6} / \boxed{3} + \boxed{2} = 4$$

24 Switching Sides

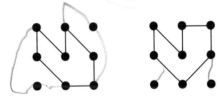

The most number of sides you can have is 7. The diagram shows two ways of reaching this total. There are many other solutions, some of which are simply rotations of the solutions above. Others involve sides consisting of more than one segment—for example, if you pushed out either lower diagonal of the right-hand figure, you would get a seven-sided figure with a squared-off corner.

25 It All Adds Up

The number is 624.

26 Don't Sneeze, Please

Nine hours is the answer. The time between the first pill and the fourth pill equals three intervals of three hours each.

27 Forever Young

The most likely explanation is that Heather was born in Australia, New Zealand, or some other place in the Southern Hemisphere, where it is winter during the months that are summer for the Northern Hemisphere. That way she could have been born in, say, July, which means that she wouldn't have reached her 40th birthday by April 2006.

28 Agent 86

32	19	27	8
10	25	17	34
9	26	18	33
35	16	24	11

29 Seeing Is Believing?

This problem is a bit of an optical illusion. The answer is line A, even though line B, at first glance, appears to be correct.

30 Five Easy Pieces

It's a trick question, of course. A square can be divided into any number of equal parts simply by drawing only vertical lines!

31 Follow the Directions

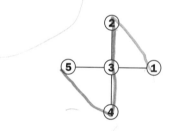

The middle number must be 3, which of course is also the middle number of 1, 2, 3, 4, and 5. The idea is that you can pair the 1 and 5 to give you a 6, and you can pair the 2 and 4 to give you another 6. But you can't pair the 3 with anything, which is why it has to go in the middle. The sum in any direction is 9. (There are four answers in all, obtained by switching the positions of the 5 and 1 or the 4 and 2.)

32 X Marks the Spot

The gray squares show two ways to add five new Xs so that every row and column has an even number of Xs.

33 The Price of Fun

The Frisbee® costs $3.70 and the softball costs $2.50. As you can see, the Frisbee® costs $1.20 more than the softball, and together they cost $6.20.

34 Fare Wars

The distance that would produce the same fare on both meters is one and a half miles. That's because the Cloud City taxi starts out more expensive by 25 cents. Every quarter-mile, the

Megalopolis taxi "makes up" five cents, so everything is even after five more quarter-miles. But don't forget the first quarter-mile, which makes six quarter-miles altogether. That's one and a half miles.

35 A Famous Triangle

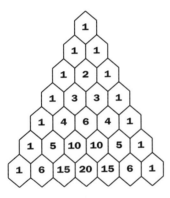

$$1 + 1 = 2$$

$$1 + 2 + 1 = 4$$

$$1 + 3 + 3 + 1 = 8$$

$$1 + 4 + 6 + 4 + 1 = 16$$

$$1 + 5 + 10 + 10 + 5 + 1 = 32$$

$$1 + 6 + 15 + 20 + 15 + 6 + 1 = 64$$

The sum of the elements of the seventh row equals 64. To get this total, you have two choices. One is to figure out the elements of the seventh row and add them all up. The other thing you can do is notice the pattern of the earlier rows. You can see that the pattern, starting with the second row, goes 2, 4, 8, 16, and so on—each new row doubles the result of the row before! Continuing all the way to the seventh row, we get the same answer: 64.

36 Magic Triangle

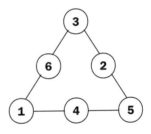

Here is one solution. Other solutions may be obtained by rotating this one to change the positions of the numbers to another side, but the position of the numbers in relation to one another doesn't change.

37 The French Connection

One way to compute the average test scores for the two students is to add up their individual test scores and divide by 5.

Average for Sandy = $(94+79+84+75+88)/5 = 420/5 = 84$

Average for Jason = $(72+85+76+81+91)/5 = 405/5 = 81$

Sandy has a three-point advantage.

An easier way might be to arrange the test scores in the following way:

Sandy: 94 88 84 79 75

Jason: 91 85 81 76 72

It is now easy to see that Sandy has a three-point advantage the whole way through, so her average must be three points higher.

38 Numbers on the House

A total of 91 numbers are required—one each for the nine houses numbered 1 through 9, and two each for the houses numbered 10 through 50.

Of these 91, each of the numbers 1 through 4 is used 15 times, the number 5 is used 6 times (the only number used this many times), and each of the numbers 6 through 0 is used 5 times. Write it out as an equation and sure enough, $(4 \times 15) + 6 + (5 \times 5) = 60 + 6 + 25 = 91$.

39 Mirror Time

The answer is 49 minutes, the time between 12:12 and 1:01.

40 Letter Perfect

ELEVEN PLUS TWO can be rearranged to spell TWELVE PLUS ONE!

41 Prime Time

32	16	24	33	45	28	54
40	23	2	11	5	19	12
14	36	10	55	17	34	49
6	50	38	13	22	51	20
21	35	3	46	27	18	39
9	29	48	15	4	52	26
55	44	25	8	42	30	1

The only one of the first ten primes that is left out of the original diagram is the number 7. But, as you can see, it makes an appearance if you shade in all the other primes.

42 The Missing Six

There is more than one answer to this puzzle. Here is one:

$$\boxed{2} + \boxed{5} = \boxed{7}$$

$$\boxed{4} - \boxed{3} = \boxed{1}$$

43 The One and Only

Forty is the number, as you can plainly see.

A B C D E **F** G H I J K L M N **O** P Q **R** S **T** U V W X **Y** Z

44 Comic Relief

One 10-ruble book, two 2-ruble books, and three 1-ruble books add up to six books and 17 rubles.

45 The Twelve Days of Christmas

The presents that show up the most are the ones given on the sixth and seventh days—the geese a-laying and the swans a-swimming. The six geese are mentioned seven times, for a total of 42, and the seven swans show up six times, again for a total of 42. (The partridge shows up the most frequently, but only one bird at a time, and the lords come around only once.)

46 Pickup Sticks

TWEN TY NINE = 29

47 Starting to Waffle

The stationary machine makes 3 waffles per second. If you used four stationary machines, you'd be making 12 waffles per second. The portable machine makes 120 waffles per minute, which is the same as 2 per second. To produce 12 waffles per second you would need 12/2 = 6 portable machines.

48 And Then There Was One

The last letter left standing is the letter W.

49 Class Dismissed

The fourth period will end at 11:55, or five minutes before noon. That's because the four class periods take up 4 x 40 = 160 minutes, while there are a total of

15 minutes between periods, 3 x 5. That's 175 minutes in all, which is just five minutes less than 180 minutes, which is three hours.

50 The Easy Way Out

(138 x 109) + (164 x 138) + (138 x 227) = 138 x (109 + 164 + 227) = 138 x 500 = 138 x 1000/2 = 138,000/2 = 69,000.

51 An Updated Classic

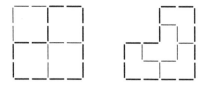

You either can add to the original diagram and create four squares, as in the left diagram, or you can separate the original shape into four identical, smaller shapes.

52 Generation Gap

Grandpa Jones is 78. His four grandchildren are 18, 19, 20, and 21. Note that 18 + 19 + 20 + 21 = 78.

In general, the sum of four consecutive numbers will never be divisible by 4. Both 76 and 80 are divisible by 4 but 78 does not share that property.

53 A Game of Chicken

Two packages of 6, three packages of 9, and three packages of 20 give you (2 x 6) + (3 x 9) + (3 x 20) = 12 + 27 + 60 = 99 McNuggets.

54 The Average Student

Three five-star homework papers will do the trick. Altogether they account for 3 x 5 = 15 stars. Adding the single star from the first homework gives 16 stars from four assignments, for an average of four stars per assignment.

Look at the problem another way. You'll see that the one-star homework paper was three stars below the desired average of four stars. Each five-star grade gains one point on the average, so it takes three assignments to balance things out.

55 Reel Life Story

There were four senior citizens in the group. They paid $3.00 apiece. The other three adults paid the full price of $6.00 per ticket, for a total of $30.00 for the seven tickets.

56 Number Path

6	7	10	11	12
5	8	9	14	13
4	1	20	15	16
3	2	19	18	17

57 Divide and Conquer

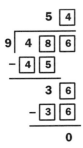

58 Apple Picking

They all cost the same!

10 apples = 1 bag (5¢) plus 3 apples at 15¢ each (45¢) = 50¢

300 apples = 4 bags (20¢) plus 2 apples at 15¢ each (30¢) = 50¢

50 apples = 7 bags (35¢) plus 1 apple at 15¢ (15¢) = 50¢

59 Squaring the Circle

When you join the diagonals of the tilted square, you also divide the outside square into four smaller squares. Then it's easy to see that the inside square contains precisely one-half of each of those smaller squares, so the tilted square must be half the size of the outside square.

60 Where's Waldo?

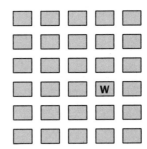

Waldo's position must be where shown in the diagram. Because each row has the same number of students, they fill up the entire 5 x 6 rectangle of seats, for 30 students in all.

61 Hundred's Place

The number 100 is found at the base of a tall column. Note that 96 is a multiple of 6, and all the multiples of 6 are located in the top spot of one of the tall columns. From there you just count a few more until getting to the magic 100.

62 The Powers of Four

Ernie came up with the number 1,048,576. Note that all of Bert's numbers end in 4, while all of Ernie's numbers end in 6. That's all you need to know!

63 Kangaroo Numbers

The kangaroo numbers on the list are 125 and 912. Note that 125 = 25 x 5, while 912 = 12 x 76.

64 Hex-a-Gone

To create a cube, separate the figure into three diamond-shaped pieces. The three lines you draw may be in the same relative positions as the ones shown, just rotated inside the hexagon—it still works. To see the cube, just tilt your head!

65 Staying in Shape

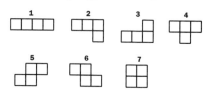

66 Oh, Brother!

The product of 8! could be written out like this:

8 x 7 x 6 x 5 x 4 x 3 x 2 x 1

And the product of 6! could look like this:

6 x 5 x 4 x 3 x 2 x 1

To solve the problem, you need to divide the product of 8! by 6!—but first, look at the two lines of numbers to see which ones they share. You can see that everything cancels out except the eight and the seven. That means 8!/6! = 8 x 7 = 56.

67 Crossing the Bridge

The one ace, three 7s, two 5s, and two 4s account for eight card s, so you only have five left (each hand has 13 cards). The greatest number of points you could have from those five cards would be 18—three aces (you already have one) and two kings. If you add those 18 points to the 4 points for the ace you already have, you would have a total of 22 points.

68 Last Train to Clarksville

It is now 4:39. Brian has to wait 9 minutes for his train to Newburgh. Amy has to wait twice that, or 18 minutes, for her train to Springfield, while Stephanie has to wait 36 minutes for her train to Clarksville.

69 How Big?

Note that the big square is divided into nine pieces: one square, four small triangles, and four odd-shaped four-sided figures (called trapezoids). Each of the four small triangles, when put together with one of the trapezoids, can easily be arranged to form a square with the same area as the central square. Since there are a total of five identical squares, the central square is therefore one-fifth the area of the larger one.

70 Putting Your Two Cents In

The pad costs 25 cents. Aaron had 23 cents and Bobby had 1 cent. Together they had 24 cents, which was a penny short.

71 Connect the Dots

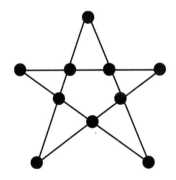

A five-pointed star does the trick.

72 Surf's Up

The original price of the surfboard was $125.00. Twenty percent is one-fifth, and one-fifth of 125 is 25. If you subtract 25 from 125, you get 100. So $100.00 is the sale price of the surfboard.

73 Square Dance

By taking out the four segments in the middle of the diagram, you reduce the number of squares from eighteen to nine (eight small squares and one big one).

74 On All Fours

$1 = (4 + 4)/(4 + 4)$ $3 = (4 + 4 + 4)/4$

$2 = (4 \times 4)/(4 + 4)$ $4 = 4 + (4 - 4)/4$

$5 = (4 \times 4 + 4)/4$ $8 = 4 + 4 + 4 - 4$

$6 = 4 + (4 + 4)/4$ $9 = 4 + 4 + 4/4$

$7 = 44/4 - 4$ $10 = (44 - 4)/4$

75 The Right Stuff

The answer is 43. Simply add up 10 + 65 + 58, getting a total of 133, then subtract 90 to get the answer. The reason this works is that when you add up 10, 65, and 58, you are "double-counting" the people with experience in both sales and publishing (the group you're interested in). So just subtract the original number of applicants (90) and you're left with the experienced people—single-counted, just the way you want!

76 Square Feet

There were 81 soldiers originally, marching in a 9 x 9 square. After 32 of them were called away, that left 49 soldiers, who then marched in a 7 x 7 square.

If not for the fact there are at least eight soldiers in the second square, there would have been a second possible solution: with 36 soldiers originally and 32 called away. Then you would have been left with 4, another perfect square!

77 Win One for the Dipper

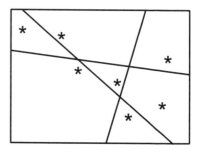

78 Trick or Treat

Mr. Greensleeve had 13 candies remaining. Note that whether you divide 13 by 2, 3, or by 4, you always get a remainder of 1. It is the only number less than 20 for which that is true.

79 Magic Circle

If you group the numbers as shown above, you can see that the sum of the numbers in each group equals 15. (4 + 5 + 6 = 15; 7 + 8 = 15; 9 + 1 + 2 + 3 = 15)

80 Jack in the Box

Suppose you number the cards 1 through 6, with the jacks being numbers 1 and 2. There are 15 different ways of selecting two cards, as follows:

1 – 2   2 – 3   3 – 4   4 – 5   5 – 6
1 – 3   2 – 4   3 – 5   4 – 6
1 – 4   2 – 5   3 – 6
1 – 5   2 – 6
1 – 6

Of these 15, only the last three columns don't contain a jack (numbered here as 1 or 2). There are six choices among those three columns, so the chance of not choosing either jack is 6/15, or 2/5. The chance of choosing at least one jack is 9/15, or 3/5, so that is the more likely event.

81 Three's a Charm

The item costs 17 cents. To purchase it requires four coins: one dime, one nickel, and two pennies. To purchase two items (34 cents) requires six coins: one quarter, one nickel, and four pennies. To purchase three items (51 cents) requires only two coins: one half-dollar and one penny.

82 Miles to Go

The gap between the two odometers is 445 miles, a gap that will not change. Therefore, the main odometer will be twice the trip odometer when the trip odometer reads 445 miles. That will happen in precisely 445 − 22 = 423 miles.

83 Stay Out of My Path!

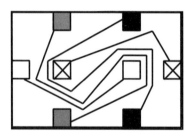

Here is one solution: Any other solutions use the same idea—you need to "wrap" two paths around one of the middle squares in order to keep from crossing lines.

84 The Run-Off

Burt should win. Why? Because when the two of them ran against Alex, Burt was exactly 20 meters ahead of Carl at the moment Alex crossed the finish line—20 meters ahead of Burt. Therefore, if Burt were to give Carl a 20-meter head start, the two of them would be even at the moment Alex crossed the finish line, when there's still 20 meters left to run. Burt is the faster runner. Therefore he would win the race—but not by much!

85 The Missing Shekel

The problem with the price of five rutabagas for two shekels is that the five rutabagas consist of 3 cheap ones (the three for a shekel variety) and 2 expensive ones (the neighbor's two for a shekel batch). By selling all 30 rutabagas in this manner, the farmer is basically selling 20 at his price and 10 at his neighbor's more expensive price—not 15 at each price. That's why he ends up a shekel short.

86 Too Close for Comfort

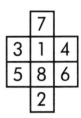

The figure here is one solution. Another can be obtained by switching the two outer "columns." In either case, the middle boxes are occupied by the 1 and the 8.

87 Donut Try This at Home

Suppose a regular donut has 100 calories. If a low-calorie donut has 95 percent fewer calories, it must have 5 calories. Therefore you must eat 20 low-calorie donuts to get as many calories as you get from one regular donut.

88 Diamond in the Rough

The only diamond card that is not symmetrical is the seven of diamonds.

89 Please Fence Me In

If you make the pen in the shape of a circle, you will get the biggest area for a given amount of fencing.

90 Misery Loves Company

Jones did worse than Smith, even after Smith's second 60% loss. To see why, assume that each man started with $1,000.00, as suggested in the hint. Then Jones ended up with $150.00, following his 85% loss. Smith had $400.00 after his first loss. After his second loss the equation becomes 400 − (60% of 400). Figure that 60% of 400 equals 240, and you'll find he ended up with the sum of 400 − 240, which comes to $160.00, barely better than Jones. The key is that Smith's second 60% loss was made on a smaller investment—$400.00 versus $1,000.00.

91 Square Route

92 Cookie Monster

Elmo's and Peter's chances are both 1/3. Clearly this is true for Elmo, because when he chooses there are three cookies, only one of which is a sugar cookie. By the time Peter chooses his cookie, he will have a chance at the sugar cookie in only two out of three cases—when Elmo hasn't already picked it! Since that means that Elmo may pick a *different* cookie two our of three times, Peter's chance at getting the sugar cookie from the two that remain will be 1/2. He'll have that chance two out of three times: 1/2 x 2/3 = 1/3.

Another way to think of the puzzle is this: Suppose there was a third person—Max—who went after Elmo and Peter. Clearly Max will get the sugar cookie whenever it is the only one left, and the chances of that happening must be 1/3. But if Elmo's chances are 1/3 and Max's chances are 1/3, the same must be true for Peter—after all, someone must get the sugar cookie!

93 Two Workers Are Better Than One

One way to solve the problem is to use fractions. The first worker completes the job in six days, so in one day he will have completed 1/6 of the total. Meanwhile, the second worker would complete 1/12 of the job in one day. Working together, they would complete 1/6 + 1/12 of the job in one day. 1/6 is the same as 2/12, so 2/12 + 1/12 = 3/12, or 1/4, which is the amount of the job they would finish in one day. So, together they would complete 1/4 of the job in one day—therefore, it will take them 4 days to get the whole job done.

If you don't want to use fractions, you can do it another way. In twelve days, the first worker would complete the entire job twice, while the second worker would complete it once. Therefore, working together, they would complete three jobs in twelve days, which is a rate of one complete job every four days (12/3 = 4).

94 Four of a Kind

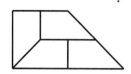

95 No Foolin'

April 1, 2001 was a Sunday. That's because one year is 365 days, or 52 weeks and one day. Any date moves ahead one day from year to year. However, in a leap year, any date after February 29 moves ahead two days. The year 2000 was a leap year, so April 1, 1999 was a Thursday.

96 A Very Good Year

The next year to have the same property will be 2307: 23 + 07 = 30.

97 Pieces of Eight

Each point from A to H (the "vertices" of the octagon) can be connected with five other points to form a diagonal. That seems to make a total of 8 x 5, or 40 diagonals. However, as it said in the hint, the diagonal from A to E is the same as the diagonal from E to A, and you can't double-count. You need to divide 40 by 2 to get the actual answer—20 diagonals.

98 Who Is the Liar?

Daniel is the liar. To see why, we examine one case at a time, using the fact that only one person is lying.

If Andrew were lying, the number would have three digits. (It couldn't have just one digit, because then it couldn't be divisible by 25, and Daniel would also be lying.) But if the number had three digits, either Barbara or Cindy would have to be lying, because 150 is the only three-digit number that goes evenly into 150. Therefore Andrew must be telling the truth, because there can only be one liar.

If Barbara were lying, then the number does not go into 150. But then either Andrew or Daniel also must be lying, because the only two-digit numbers that are divisible by 25 (25, 50, and 75) all go evenly into 150. So Barbara must be telling the truth.

If Cindy were lying, then the number would be 150. But then Andrew also would have to be lying, because 150 has three digits, not two.

So, the only possibility left is that Daniel is the liar, and this works out. If the number were 10, for example, Daniel would be lying, but the other three statements would all be true.

99 Playing the Triangle

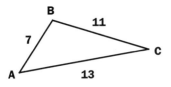

The key to this puzzle is that if you add up the lengths of any two sides of any triangle, the sum must be greater than the third side. Why is this true? Because the shortest distance between any two points is a straight line. For example, in the diagram below, AB + BC could never be less than AC, because then an indirect route from A to C—stopping off at B along the way—

would be shorter than the direct route!

What this means is that 5 cannot be the third side, because 5 + 7 < 13. In the same way, 21 is impossible, because 7 + 13 < 21. That leaves 11 as the only possible answer.

100 House of Cards

There are nine same-size cards with a total area of 180, so each one must have an area of 20. The measurements of each card are therefore 4 x 5 (note that 4 x 5 = 20), and the length of four cards in the diagram is precisely equal to the width of five cards. If each card is 4 x 5, the height of the figure is nine inches and the length is 20 inches, so the perimeter equals 2 x (20 + 9) = 58 inches.

··· Index ···